HAMBURG

THE CITY AT A GLANCE

Binnenalster

The 'inner' lake is actually a man-m~~ade~~
reservoir. Its shores are Hamburg's
playground and the venue for large-
events and festivals.

Fairmont Hotel Vier Jahreszeiten

Dating from 1897 and extended in the 1930s
and the 1950s, the 'Four Seasons' is one of the
grandest of the fin-de-siècle white mansions
that line the shores of Binnenalster.
See p016

Rathaus

The city hall, a rambling neo-Renaissance
structure completed in 1897, is the focal point
of Mitte. Its elaborate façade features 20
busts of the kaisers and a riot of adornment.
See p015

HafenCity

Although only the first phase is complete,
this ambitious docklands redevelopment has
already changed the landscape of the city
and attracted the world's architectural élite.
See p026

Congress Centrum Hamburg

The central location of Hamburg's trade-fair
buildings is a big draw, and the facilities have
recently been expanded. The main exhibition
hall features a 8,000 sq m roof garden.
See p014

Michaeliskirche

The 82m bell tower and distinctive clock face
of this much-loved city icon are said to have
guided sailors to the city's shores. The views
from the top are wonderful.
See p009

INTRODUCTION

THE CHANGING FACE OF THE URBAN SCENE

Bourgeois, cosmopolitan and just a little aloof, Hamburg is not an in-your-face kind of town, a fact many credit to its booming professional population – locals would rather spend an extra hour on their Macs than on the subway. For the visitor, this does mean that a little creative tourism is needed. But if you take your time and dig below the surface, it'll soon become apparent why few Germans love their city as much as Hamburgers do theirs.

Its location between the Elbe and Alster rivers, expanses of greenery, deep blue lakes and pleasant canals certainly make Hamburg a beautiful city. It's also one of Europe's wealthiest, its millionaires still filling their coffers thanks to the tax-free status of its port. Unlike many other European cities, which for years turned their backs on their docklands (a trend that has only lately been reversed), Hamburgers have always embraced theirs, while the Elbe has accommodated their history's ebb and flow.

Today, Hamburg is Germany's media capital, and home to the HQs of publishing giants such as *Stern*, *Die Zeit* and *Spiegel*. Rather than losing residents, as it did for much of the early 20th century, the city is now gaining them, with the population expected to rise 16 per cent by 2040. HafenCity (see p026), the massive waterside urban development, due for completion by 2025, has largely been conceived to accommodate these new urban immigrants, and is a blank canvas that is attracting many of the world's top architects.

ESSENTIAL INFO

FACTS, FIGURES AND USEFUL ADDRESSES

TOURIST OFFICE
Hamburg Tourismus
Kirchenallee
Hauptbahnhof
T 3005 1300
www.hamburg-tourism.de

TRANSPORT
Car hire
Avis
T 5075 2314
Europcar
T 2364 8560
Taxis
Hamburger Taxi
T 311 311
Water taxis
Hadag
St Pauli Fischmarkt 28
T 311 7070
www.hadag.de
Bike rental
Der Fahrradladen
Barnerstrasse 28
T 390 3824
www.derfahrradladenaltona.de

EMERGENCY SERVICES
Ambulance/Fire
T 112
Police
T 110

CONSULATES
British Consulate
Harvestehuder Weg 8a
T 448 0320
www.britischebotschaft.de
US Consulate
Alsterufer 27/28
T 4117 1100
hamburg.usconsulate.gov

MONEY
American Express
T 069 9797 1000
travel.americanexpress.com

POSTAL SERVICES
Post Office
Kirchenallee
Hauptbahnhof
Shipping
UPS
T 0800 882 6630
www.ups.com

BOOKS
Hamburg: Building for the Growing City (Jovis Verlag)
On the Natural History of Destruction by WG Sebald (Hamish Hamilton)
The Beatles in Hamburg by Jürgen Vollmer (Schirmer/Mosel Verlag)

WEBSITES
Architecture
www.archinform.net
Magazine and Newspapers
hamburg.prinz.de
www.hamburgnews.com
www.spiegel.de/international

COST OF LIVING
Taxi from Hamburg Airport to city centre
£17.50
Cappuccino
£2
Packet of cigarettes
£2.60
Daily newspaper
£1
Bottle of champagne
£38.50

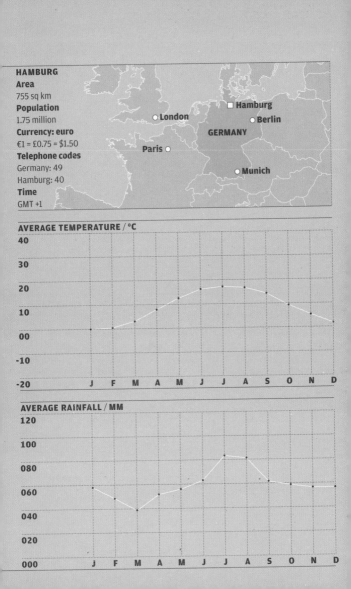

HAMBURG
Area
755 sq km
Population
1.75 million
Currency: euro
€1 = £0.75 = $1.50
Telephone codes
Germany: 49
Hamburg: 40
Time
GMT +1

London
Hamburg
Berlin
GERMANY
Paris
Munich

AVERAGE TEMPERATURE / °C

40
30
20
10
00
-10
-20

J F M A M J J A S O N D

AVERAGE RAINFALL / MM

120
100
080
060
040
020
000

J F M A M J J A S O N D

NEIGHBOURHOODS

THE AREAS YOU NEED TO KNOW AND WHY

To help you navigate the city, we've chosen the most interesting districts (see below and the map inside the back cover) and colour-coded our featured venues, according to their location; those venues that are outside these areas are not coloured.

EIMSBÜTTEL

Park-filled, residential Eimsbüttel has begun to benefit from the overflow of hip 'hoods Schanze and St Pauli. The NDR broadcasting station is located just to the north, and media agencies have followed its lead, setting up around Weidenallee, which is a great café and shopping strip.

ST GEORG

This friendly, villagey gay district boasts shops, clubs and cinemas clustered around Steindamm, while Lange Reihe hosts a stream of cafés, designer shops and bars amid red-brick residences. Aussenalster lake demarcates the north-west edge, skirted by An der Alster, home to exclusive boat clubs and gracious white mansions.

MITTE WEST

Binnenalster lake is the focal point of the blue-blood swathe of the city centre. Other draws are the Italianate Alsterarkaden, its graceful arches providing shelter to high-end shops and terrace cafés, and the huge Planten un Blomen park to the north, which is a triumph of botanical design.

EPPENDORF AND HARVESTEHUDE

Bourgeois Eppendorf offers upmarket retail therapy along Eppendorfer Baum; while on Isestrasse, the city's finest white classical and neo-baroque mansions are the backdrop to a great food market. Early 20th-century splendour can be seen along Hochallee in Harvestehude.

HAFENCITY

Cranes, canals and cutting-edge, big-name architecture mark this docklands project that is finding new uses for century-old red-brick and gabled warehouses. For example, Herzog & de Meuron's Elbphilharmonie (due 2010) places an iceberg-like structure on top of a massive quay warehouse.

SCHANZE

Often considered to be the northern part of St Pauli, Schanze, which encompasses Schanzenviertel and Karolinenviertel, is a pocket of left-of-centre hipness. Funky food outlets and fashion start-ups line Marktstrasse and its cross streets, while Sternschanzenpark hosts the Mövenpick Hotel (see p016) in a converted water tower.

MITTE EAST

East of the Alsterfleet canal lies the city's retail hub and the grandiose Rathaus (see p015). Further east, in Kontorhausviertel, there are fine examples of 1920s vernacular clinker-brick office buildings, including the Chilehaus (see p013) and the neighbouring Sprinkenhof and Mohlenhof (Burchardplatz).

ALTONA AND ST PAULI

There's more to this area than the infamous Reeperbahn. Striking public spaces and new architecture, such as Dockland (see p010), are springing up beside the Elbe. Chilled-out, multicultural Altona, with its gourmet food shops and cafés, is in stark contrast to its gritty, rock'n'roll neighbour, St Pauli.

LANDMARKS
THE SHAPE OF THE CITY SKYLINE

The waterways of Hamburg are its signposts. The sparkling blue of the Binnenalster lake forms the northern boundary of Mitte East and West, the historic centre that is dominated by the opulent Rathaus (see p015). The Alsterfleet canal divides Mitte into its two halves and the Elbe river marks the centre's southern edge. However, the mammoth HafenCity (see p026) project, which is being built in stages, will annex the old warehouse district on an island in the Elbe to the city proper, expanding the centre of Hamburg by 40 per cent. Workers in Mitte will then have a mere 10-minute walk past the famous Chilehaus (see p013) to reach their designer lofts in the new 'Harbour City'.

Waterside development is also being embraced further east. Dockland (see p010) is the modern beacon for the old port, an industrial swathe of land where fish-packing warehouses sit beside (or house) stylish new restaurants such as Henssler & Henssler (see p038). Inland are the hip, left-field neighbourhoods of Altona and St Pauli. Approaching from Mitte, it is often claimed that Michaeliskirche (Englische Planke 1a, T 376 780) is the gateway to Hamburg's famous red-light district, but it's not until you can see the soaring concrete walls of the WWII bunker Flakturm IV (see p012) to the north that you are entering this must-see part of St Pauli, where the action clusters around its main drag, Reeperbahn. *For full addresses, see Resources.*

Dockland

Built entirely on the water by Hamburg
architects Bothe Richter Teherani, this
sloping steel-and-glass office building
projects 40m over the river like a ship's
prow. Worth the climb is the rooftop
terrace, which boasts great views of the
waterside and the Elbberg Campus (see
p062), also by Bothe Richter Teherani.
Van-der-Smissen-Strasse 9,
www.dockland-hamburg.de

Flakturm IV

The monolithic Flakturm IV is one of the eight Flak towers (anti-aircraft-gun blockhouses that also acted as shelters) commissioned by the Third Reich during WWII. Hitler's engineering team, the Organisation Todt, took bunker design to a new level and considered the buildings impenetrable (they were largely correct). Built in pairs (Flakturm IV's twin was later demolished), each tower provided a separate base for attack and command with underground cables linking the two. About 18,000 people could take shelter behind the 3.5m-thick concrete walls of Flakturm IV, which had its own water and electricity supplies and hospital. Today, you will find recording studios and the popular live music venue Uebel & Gefährlich (www.uebelundgefaehrlich.com) inside.
Feldstrasse 66

Chilehaus

Fritz Höger's building is the most famous of Hamburg's unique *Kontorhäuser* (office buildings). It was built in 1924 for Henry B Sloman, a successful importer of nitrate from Chile, on two irregularly shaped plots. Höger's solution was a graciously pointed, 10-storey, ship-like landmark that became a symbol of Hamburg itself. Indeed, the daring shape inspired the logo of the city's 'Summer of Architecture' in 2003. Nearly five million red-and-violet-hued clinker brinks were used to create Höger's structure, which today houses private apartments and offices. Perhaps the most spectacular feature is the courtyard and its archway entrances, which act as a gateway from the city's original merchants' quarter to the *Speicherstadt* (warehouse district). *Fischertwiete 2, www.chilehaus.de*

Congress Centrum Hamburg

Jost Schramm and Gerd Pempelfort's CCH was 10 years in development, but with the help of town planner Ernst May, Germany's first congress centre opened in 1973 with the then Plaza Hotel towering over it. Already one of Europe's largest conference venues, it was recently expanded with a massive glass-and-steel extension designed by Brauer Architekten on the edge of the Planten un Blomen botanical gardens.

The lower floors of Schramm and Pempelfort's radical masterpiece haven't been abandoned, though, and still house smaller trade fairs. Meanwhile, the Top of Town Bar & Lounge on the 26th and 27th floors of what is now the Radisson SAS Hotel (T 3502 3400) has giddy views. *Marseiller Strasse 1, T 35 690, www.cch.de*

Rathaus

After the great fire of 1842 destroyed Hamburg's first town hall, it took the city authorities more than 50 years to replace it. Architect Martin Haller, who also designed the gracious white mansion on Aussenalster lake that now serves as the US consulate, headed the Bund der Rathausbaumeister (Group of Town Hall Building Masters) and came up with a rambling neo-Renaissance design that tour guides love to boast (wrongly) has more rooms than Buckingham Palace. The massive castle-like form features fairytale spikes and pinnacles, and inside, the splendid vestibule is embellished with marble walls and brass inlay. Join a tour to see the great debating hall and opulent banquet rooms, before heading outside to Rathausmarkt, the heart of old Hamburg. *Rathausmarkt 1, T 428 312 064*

HOTELS

WHERE TO STAY AND WHICH ROOMS TO BOOK

It took a major sporting event for Hamburg to enter into the consciousness of the world traveller. Since 2006, when the city was one of the hosts of the World Cup, tourism has grown by 5.5 per cent, a figure that is only expected to rise. Hamburg's hotel scene has responded, with design teams making their mark on the accommodation on offer. Standouts include the Park Hyatt (Bugenhagenstrasse 8, T 3332 1234), located in the Levantehaus, a 1912 merchants' building, East (see p021), 25hours (opposite) and Side (see p020), and the budget options YoHo (Moorkamp 5, T 284 1910) and Hotel York (Hofweg 19, T 227 1420), which both combine art nouveau architecture with contemporary interiors.

At the other end of the scale, the city's grande dames, such as the Fairmont Hotel Vier Jahreszeiten (Neuer Jungfernstieg 9-14, T 34 940), offer lake views and fin-de-siècle splendour, but few nods to contemporary hotel culture, bar wi-fi. For the best of both worlds, the Mövenpick Hotel (Sternschanze 6, T 334 4110) and the Gastwerk (see p023) are both cutting-edge hotels in converted landmarks, a water tower and gasworks respectively. Quirkier options include Cap San Diego (Überseebrücke, T 364 209), which offers eight 'cabins' in an anchored vessel, while the chintzy décor of Hotel Village (Steindamm 4, T 480 6490) has changed little from the days when it was a high-class bordello.

For full addresses and room rates, see Resources.

25hours

The hip younger sister of the Gastwerk Hotel (see p023), 25hours is the perfect boutique option. The lipstick-pink circular reception desk sets the tone for the irreverent interiors by Evi Märklstetter and Armin Fischer. Though the rooms, such as the Large Standard (above), are not spacious, they are bathed in soothing white, with slate floors, curved furniture, powder-blue walls and shag rugs. The room-service concept has been replaced by chilled-out common spaces – a lobby bar, restaurant, rooftop terrace and event area – and don't be surprised to see a fashion shoot going on. Just as stylish are the staff, who are only too eager to point you towards Altona's best-kept secrets. Reserve Room 500 for the big balcony. *Paul-Dessau-Strasse 2, T 855 070, www.25hours-hotel.com*

Hotel Atlantic Kempinski
Perhaps not the grandest of Hamburg's
grande dames, but majestic all the same,
the Kempinski has accommodated Edith
Piaf and Madonna. The front rooms have
windows overlooking the Aussen-Alster
lake and charming old-school details; the
sleek, monochrome BMW Suite (pictured)
is the most contemporary option.
An der Alster 72-79, T 28 880,
www.kempinski.atlantic.de

Side

Of all the city's design hotels, Side has the most remarkable lobby (above): an atrium-like glass-and-stone space that rises up to the eighth floor. Located near the posh shops on Jungfernstieg, this is a party hotel, and its clientele, a smattering of intercontinental weekenders and media types, reflects this. The rooms offer cream and beige furnishings offset by crayon-coloured details and dark wood flooring and, as a surprise touch, square toilet seats. The Executive Suites (especially 1109 with its lake view) have generous wardrobes and walk-through bathrooms. Other assets are the Side Spa and the sweeping view from the sun terrace. *Drehbahn 49, T 309 990, www.side-hamburg.de*

East

Chicago-based architect Jordan Mozer has instilled his singular vision in an old iron foundry, creating an arresting space that offers eye candy at every turn. The 125 rooms, lofts and suites, such as the East Apartment (above), are spread out over the original building, while an annex lies beyond an outdoor garden. The addition of the in-house Yakshi's Bar and East Restaurant (see p042) make the hotel feel more like an urban club than a hotel. In some rooms, norms governing layout are thrown out the window; for instance, organic-shaped beds are placed at right angles in the middle of the floor. Standard Room 116 has a small private terrace.
Simon-von-Utrecht-Strasse 31, T 309 930, www.east-hamburg.de

Hotel Wedina

The Wedina is all about home comforts. It's divided between four apartment buildings in a quiet residential street, and each one has a different colour and a theme. The original Blue House is devoted to the written word, and established authors who agree to a reading get to stay in its simply furnished rooms for free. The Yellow House embraces the sun, with its Mediterranean-style décor, terraces and family apartments. The latest addition is the Green House, which was conceived for the design-hungry traveller. Rooms, such as 312 (above), feature Scandinavian styling, a glass façade, split-level rooms, a workstation and pretty views.
*Gurlittstrasse 23, T 280 8900,
www.wedina.de*

Gastwerk Hotel

The slightly out-of-the-way location does not stop design junkies flocking here. As the name suggests, it is located in an old gasworks, which has been converted into a sophisticated hotel incorporating original features from the 1896 building. In the common areas, exposed brick walls are complemented by burnt orange and brown furniture, while iron beams support the high white walls of the atrium/lobby.

The rooms and suites offer delightfully comfortable beds and sofas, and many have arched windows. For loft-style living, book a Junior Suite in the tower, the top-floor Conran Shop Suite (above) or the Penthouse Suite, which has a terrace.
Beim Alten Gaswerk 3, Daimlerstrasse, T 890 620, www.gastwerk.com

24 HOURS

SEE THE BEST OF THE CITY IN JUST ONE DAY

One element that you can't escape in Hamburg is water. Unlike the notoriously wet weather, its lakes, harbour and rivers are its pride and joy. The elegant Jungfernstieg along the Binnenalster offers lovely viewpoints, as well as cafés in which to kickstart your day, such as Dat Backhus (opposite). From here, navigate the bridges of Mitte to reach the *Speicherstadt* (warehouse quarter). These red-brick buildings were constructed between 1885 and 1912, and form the most architecturally coherent of Hamburg's old districts. Creeping up on its threshold is HafenCity (see po26), where a must-view is the under-construction Elbphilharmonie (Am Kaiserkai) designed by Herzog & de Meuron. A giant model of the area can be seen at the InfoCenter (see po26).

On a rainy day, take in an exhibition along the Kunstmeile (see po28) and then, over tea, revel in the old-world splendour of the Fairmont Hotel Vier Jahreszeiten (see po16) or the Lime Tree Terrace (see po30). If the sun is out, take a steamship tour with Alster Touristik (Anleger Jungfernstieg, T 357 4240) from April to October, or jump on a launch through the docks with Hadag (Pier 2, St Pauli Landungsbrücken, T 311 7070). End the day with a cocktail by the lake at A Mora (see po46) or at one of the city's best beach clubs, Strandperle (Schulberg, T 880 1112), from April to September, and then dinner at Bistrot Vienna (see po31). *For full addresses, see Resources.*

09.00 Dat Backhus

This chain of venues for the Dat Backhus group, by Hamburg-based architect André Poitiers, has won numerous awards and been featured in many design books. So, as you are sipping your latte and eating the best croissants and *Franzbrötchen* (a local cinnamon-filled speciality) in town, consider the stainless-steel fittings, the horizontal lighting over the display areas, the bold signage and the urban feel that Poitiers has lent to the normally homespun bakery. Each branch is slightly different, and the Jungfernstieg one in Hamburg's commercial heart is spread out over two storeys. Buy pastries to go from the downstairs counter, or take them upstairs to the sleek eating area (above). *Jungfernstieg 45, T 789 770*

11.00 HafenCity

The sheer scope of this waterfront development – not to mention its solid financial backing from both government and private enterprise – has attracted architects such as Rem Koolhaas, David Chipperfield and Herzog & de Meuron. It will not be finished until the 2020s, but you can explore Sandtorkai (pictured), the first district to be completed.

InfoCenter, Am Sandtorkai 30, T 3690 1799

13.00 Kunstmeile

From HafenCity, it's a short walk to the city's 'Art Mile', or museum belt. In the Hamburger Kunsthalle (T 4281 31200), the largest of the country's galleries outside Berlin, you can view European works from the 14th century onwards, or skip straight to the contemporary works, by artists such as Georg Baselitz and Gerhard Richter, in the adjacent Galerie der Gegenwart. Smaller, more avant-garde venues in the area include the Freie Akademie der Künste (T 324 632), run by a collective of artists and performers, and, in the same building, the Kunstverein (T 338 344). The Deichtorhallen (above; T 321 030) is an acclaimed photography and contemporary art gallery located in two former markets. On the ground floor, the Fillet of Soul bistro (T 7070 5800) is highly recommended for lunch.

16.00 Lime Tree Terrace

Twenty minutes out of town, on the banks of the Elbe, the Hotel Louis C Jacob has one of the most famous bars in the country. The German Impressionist Max Liebermann lived at the hotel in the summer of 1902 and often painted the leafy café terrace that overlooks the river. The most famous painting, *Terrasse im Restaurant Jacob in Nienstedten an der Elbe*, hangs in the city's Kunsthalle (see p028) and depicts well-to-do families being served tea underneath the café's forest of lime trees. Creating a modern version of this idyllic scene would require minimum effort, as little has changed except the tables and the menu, which now includes cocktails and spirits. It's a lovely spot for afternoon tea, which is served here on warm days.
Elbchaussee 401-403, T 822 550, www.hotel-jacob.de

20.00 Bistrot Vienna

A favourite topic for food bloggers, dinner here is a memorable experience. Bistrot Vienna is located in a tiny space (it can only seat 30 at a time) on a residential street, and the wooden tables are so close together that communication with fellow diners is unavoidable (an outdoor terrace in the summer provides some breathing space). Forget any calorie counting and tuck in to the creative, seasonal food on offer, such as pickled herrings with mango chutney, avocado and poppadoms. As you are eating dessert — for example, berry fruits baked in mascarpone — chef/owner Sven Bunge will invariably pop out of the rear kitchen and strike up a conversation. Afterwards, take your coffee at the front bar, where locals enjoy a late-night natter.
Fettstrasse 2, T 439 9182, www.vienna-hamburg.de

URBAN LIFE
CAFÉS, RESTAURANTS, BARS AND NIGHTCLUBS

Port cities usually produce colourful nightlife, and Hamburg is no exception. Mix together a healthy alternative scene, an appreciation of design, a varied cuisine that doesn't shy from other cultures, a host of live-music venues and the most infamous red-light district in Europe, and you have a cocktail that's hard to beat.

For a night of slumming it par excellence, the Reeperbahn in St Pauli still delivers. Everybody comes here, from designer-clad ad execs to black-clad goths and groups of curious tourists. The city's main music venue is <u>Grosse Freiheit 36</u> (T 3177 7811), which has a line-up of international acts and DJs. There are also countless bars and clubs along the length of *Die sündige Meile* (The Sinful Mile). Less salacious are the <u>Betty Ford Klinik</u> (Grosse Freiheit 6) and the <u>Golden Pudel Club</u> (Fischmarkt 27, T 3197 9930). Or take a taxi further west to the stylish <u>Club La Nuit</u> (see p052), nestled among a clutch of good restaurants on the Altona waterfront.

Hamburg claims to be the gastronomic centre of the country, and certainly in terms of variety, it excels. For indigenous fare, try the charming <u>Bistrot Vienna</u> (see p031), or <u>Oberhafen-Kantine</u> (Stockmeyerstrasse 39, T 9823 5615), which is run by the mother of Tim Mälzer, who is Germany's answer to Jamie Oliver. He has his own riverside place, Das Weisse Haus (Neumühlen 50, T 390 9016), but you'll need to book well in advance to get a table. *For full addresses, see Resources.*

Die Herren Simpel

This calming, fuss-free café is one of the few in this neck of the woods to have a rear garden, a theme it references inside with a pretty floral mural behind the bar (above), and distressed outdoor furniture elsewhere. Come here for breakfast, which, conveniently for late risers, is served until 3pm, and try a hangover-curing German special: several types of bread, salami and cheese. At other times of the day, cakes and coffee are served to customers who while away the time with a good book. The vibe changes dramatically after 7pm, when the cocktail menu comes out, and locals pop in for a pick-me-up of Aperol, the Italian aperitif, and lime.
Schulterblatt 75, T 3868 4600,
www.dieherrensimpel.de

Café Paris

Reassuringly, this gorgeous Jugendstil relic hasn't been taken over by tourists; locals are just as likely to be taking their morning coffee at the bar or sipping a pastis on the small terrace, which has a splendid view of the Rathaus (see p015). Inside, white-aproned waiters serve French bistro staples, such as steak frites. *Rathaustrasse 4, T 3252 7777, www.cafeparis.net*

Tide

Chef Frank Walbeck combines both his passions – driftwood and food – at this serene café. When you arrive, Walbeck will often be peeling a bucketful of berries he has collected himself, which he then takes into his tiny back kitchen to slow cook and turn into jams. Beautifully bottled preserves, as well as olive oils and vinegars are sold here, and all make great gifts to take home (the Tide Kit, a seasonal box containing cake, jam and sweets, is especially covetable). You can also enjoy superior coffee, homemade cakes and freshly prepared sandwiches on the premises. When Walbeck is not in the kitchen, he is scouting deserted beaches in Denmark for driftwood, which he then sells as artwork – his pieces are dotted about the café and shop.
Rathestrasse 53, T 4111 1499, www.tide.dk

Henssler & Henssler

In a city with a constant supply of high-quality fresh fish, sushi is popular. This spacious old packing warehouse by the fish market has been converted into a stylish restaurant by Werner Henssler and his son, Steffen, a celebrity chef who studied the art of sushi in LA. Consequently, the restaurant is firmly of the Californian fusion school. Although classic Japanese tempura and sashimi are available, specials are made with the day's catch. Whether you choose to dine on the outdoor terrace overlooking the port and the nearby Dockland (see p010) building, in the simply adorned wood dining room or in the rear sushi bar, it's best to book ahead. This is generally considered the best place in town in which to wave your chopsticks.
Grosse Elbstrasse 160, T 3869 9000, www.h2dine.de

Cox Restaurant

If it weren't for the German-language menu, you could swear you were in Paris, as Cox out-bistros much of what passes for one in the French capital. Bentwood chairs and cracked leather banquettes are spread out over a split-level space (ask to be seated in the front room, which looks out onto the busy Lange Reihe), and the waiting staff are as handsome as the low-lit interior. After choosing a bottle from the succinct list of European wines, try the clear beetroot soup with dumplings and chanterelles, followed by the veal carpaccio topped with black truffle and pecorino. Cox is located near Hamburg's theatre district and it is a post-performance supper favourite with local thespians, so it gets rather lively. *Lange Reihe 68, T 249 422, www.restaurant-cox.de*

R&B

Advertising and media professionals head to this restaurant for its home-cooked lunch and laid-back vibe, plus the chance to leaf through the latest design and pop culture magazines at the front bar. The name says it all: black-and-white portraits of classic jazz and blues artists line the walls, juxtaposed with florid lampshades and even a miniature Chinese temple. The cuisine is focused on local dishes, such as Gänsekeule (goose drumstick with berry sauce), but occasionally the chef will whip up a Cajun classic like jambalaya. At night, Billie Holiday croons over the sound system as locals pile in for a cocktail or dinner. *Weidenallee 20, T 441 044*

Yakshi's Bar and East Restaurant

The bar at the East hotel (see p021) is a destination in its own right, and a separate entrance ensures you never feel as if you are drinking in a lobby. Jordan Mozer's design is breathtaking, with white globular teardrops hanging over the bar, oversized organic-shaped furniture and giant bone-like structures set within the brick walls of this former iron foundry. The restaurant (above), with its simple furniture and large windows overlooking the garden, is a little more restrained, though the menu makes up for that with fussy concoctions, such as marinated saddle of veal, Franco-Japanese sushi cloud and miso fig-mustard jus. If that sounds too much of a mouthful, then just chill out at the bar, which offers a solid range of cocktails and sushi.
Simon-von-Utrecht-Strasse 31, T 309 933, www.east-hamburg.de

Tarantella

Close to the Staatsoper (see p064), this restaurant serves first-class European cuisine in a stylish interior. If you feel like a light lunch or post-work cocktail, the front bistro bar with its open kitchen is the place to be. But for something more upmarket, book the middle room (above), which has leather banquettes, or the rear dining room, a striking area with seating for 15 (it can be used for private meetings) that is dominated by heavy burnt-orange drapes and a Murano chandelier. Baby lamb roasted in rosemary and thyme or the truffle cannelloni are recommended, and the wine list is excellent, with local Rieslings and bottles from Chile and New Zealand. In good weather, you can dine on the outside terrace with its park views. *Stephansplatz 10, T 6506 7790, www.tarantella.cc*

Tafelhaus

Chef Christian Rachs' Tafelhaus is generally considered to be the best restaurant in the city and has earned him a Michelin star. A pared-down, glass-enclosed culinary temple with a wooden terrace, it has a superb view of the harbour. The creative cuisine spans Mediterranean and Asian flavours. *Neumühlen 17, T 892 760, www.tafelhaus.de*

A Mora

Hamburg revels in its lakes. The smaller Binnenalster acts as a focal point and, thanks to development on Jungfernstieg, has plenty of terraces and benches from which to admire the Geneva-style geyser in its centre. The larger Aussenalster (it takes three hours to walk around) is more bucolic, and a millionaire's row skirts its shores. But you don't have to be one to enjoy the outdoor bars on the edge of the brilliant-blue water. You need to be quick, though, as on sunny days, beautiful locals head here in droves for a sunset cocktail. The place to be seen is A Mora, a sleek, monochrome bar on a jetty, with sunbeds and a laid-back soundtrack.
An der Alster, T 2805 6846, www.a-mora.com

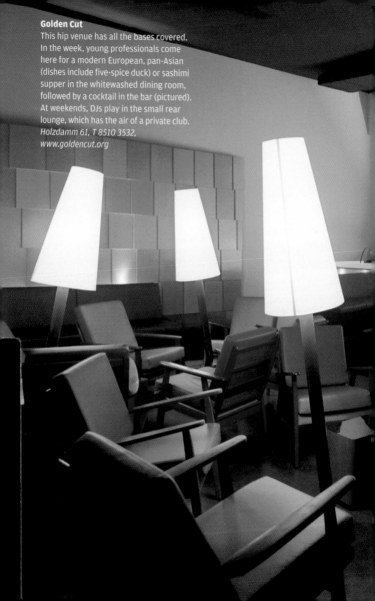

Golden Cut
This hip venue has all the bases covered.
In the week, young professionals come
here for a modern European, pan-Asian
(dishes include five-spice duck) or sashimi
supper in the whitewashed dining room,
followed by a cocktail in the bar (pictured).
At weekends, DJs play in the small rear
lounge, which has the air of a private club.
Holzdamm 61, T 8510 3532,
www.goldencut.org

Bar Rossi

This was the first St Pauli bar to offer a stylish alternative to the often sleazy scene along Reeperbahn – a fact locals and visiting VIPs appreciate by never letting Bar Rossi slip in popularity. Come here for its dramatic city views, high ceilings, plush seating, outdoor terrace and laid-back, lounge-lizard vibe.
Max-Brauer-Allee 279, T 433 421, www.bar-rossi.eu

Club La Nuit

Berlin studio 3deluxe-Biorhythm wanted
to emphasise the harbourside location
when it designed this shipshape nightclub
(open Thursday-Saturday). Large windows
overlook Dockland (see p010), and the
striated interior, in teak, cream leather
and white Corian, calls to mind a luxury
yacht. Arrive early to bag one of the
sofas facing the water. The DJs — booked
by German record producer Mousse T's
company, Peppermint Jam — spin house,
soul or R'n'B, and to ensure a multisensory
experience for the upmarket, over-30s
crowd, the place is awash with computer-
programmed lighting. Meanwhile, films
are projected across a 16m-wide window
span that separates the club from its
sister restaurant, Au Quai (3803 7730).
The latter offers contemporary global
cuisine and an appealing riverside terrace.
Grosse Elbstrasse 145d, T 3803 7731,
www.au-quai.de

INSIDER'S GUIDE

CHRISTOPHER PATTERSON, WINDOW DISPLAY DESIGNER

American-born, Hamburg-bred Christopher Patterson is an events and window-display designer, who lends his artistic hand to posh shops in the Eimsbüttel district and society weddings all over the country. He starts the day with a *galão* (milky coffee) and *pastéis de nata* (Portuguese custard tarts), which he says are 'the best in town', at Pastelaria Caravela (Lange Reihe 13, T 412 999), close to where he lives in St Georg. When not working, he likes to cycle around HafenCity to check on its progress, dropping into Oberhafen-Kantine (see p032) for a lunch of meatballs and potato salad, or going to see exhibitions at the cutting-edge Deichtorhallen (see p028). Sourcing objects for his work often takes him to boho Karolinenviertel's 'little shops with hidden gems'. He stocks up on gourmet goodies at Mutterland (Ernst-Merck-Strasse 9, T 2840 7944) and Claus Kröger (Grosse Bergstrasse 241, T 380 6060).

On grey Sundays, he has brunch at Vapiano (Hohe Bleichen 10, T 3501 9975), a stylish, self-serve bistro, where he recommends the tagliatelle carbonara. When the sun is out, Patterson likes to head to A Mora (see p046) for a post-work cocktail next to the lake. His favourite restaurant is Cox (see p039), 'because it's so different for Hamburg', and after dinner there he may stroll to the nearby M&V Gaststätte (Lange Reihe 22, T 3170 6180) to enjoy a Kölsch beer in its authentic wooden *kneipe* (tavern) interior.

For full addresses, see Resources.

ARCHITOUR

A GUIDE TO HAMBURG'S ICONIC BUILDINGS

Hamburg's architectural allure lies in its contrasts. The future is HafenCity (see p026), which aims to become a 'city within a city'. The first residents have moved in, to the Am Sandtorkai quarter, located next to Hamburg's late 19th-century warehouses, and with 1.8 million sq m of floor space to be built, it's a safe bet that most architectural practices in the city will eventually be involved.

Although Hamburg suffered widespread bomb damage during WWII, it's possible to get a glimpse of its distinctive prewar look. The clinker-brick tradition survived longer in northern Germany than in the rest of the country, and the best examples, such as the Chilehaus (see p013), can be seen in Kontorhausviertel (the office district), just north of HafenCity. Art nouveau buildings fared less well, though glimpses of Jugendstil architecture can be found wedged between the steel-and-glass towers in Mitte and, more coherently, north-west of the Aussenalster in Eppendorf.

Today, the local studio BRT (Bothe, Richter and Teherani) is a key presence in the city, with major works, such as the Dockland building (see p010), Elbberg Campus (see p062) and Habitat (see p066) clustered in Altona, and the oval, aluminium-and-glass-fronted HQ of the lighting designer Tobias Grau (Siemensstrasse 35b, T 013 700) in the north. Contact A-tour (Lutterothstrasse 23, T 2393 9717) for city-wide architectural guides.

For full addresses, see Resources.

Köhlbrandbrücke

To see this marvel of modern engineering up close, you'll need a car or a water taxi: the Köhlbrandbrücke has only been opened to pedestrians twice since it was unveiled in 1974. Designed by the architect Egon Jux, who is also responsible for the Grand Duchess Charlotte Bridge in Luxembourg, it connects the harbour with the north and south branches of the Elbe. It is the largest of Hamburg's 2,300 bridges, and it took 12,700 tonnes of steel to form its 75 supporting pylons and 88 steel cables. At almost 4km long and 55m high, the bridge is a soaring example of cable-stayed design.
A7 Autobahn, Waltershof

ADA 1

The paint is barely dry on this exciting new building, but it has already earned an assured place on the Aussenalster waterfront. It was designed by Berlin-based architects Jürgen Mayer H, whose combination of new technology and creativity has garnered them a string of awards. The An der Alster office complex stands between dense, downtown Hamburg and the lakes, and its sinuous curves sit beautifully in its park-like setting. Distinctive oval windows house meeting rooms, and provide a generous source of light. More of Jürgen Mayer H's cutting-edge work can be seen in construction near HafenCity (Steckelhoern 11), where they have positioned an almost impossibly dimensioned, vertical office block between two historic buildings.
An der Alster 1, www.jmayerh.de

Polizeirevier Davidwache
This well-loved Hamburg landmark was
designed by Fritz Schumacher, the city
planner and co-founder of the Deutscher
Werkbund group, an alliance of architects
and craftsmen who advocated a mix of
industrial and artisanal methods. The
police station has reigned over Hamburg's
den of iniquity, the Reeperbahn, since
1914, and even became the subject of
a 1964 film directed by Jürgen Roland.
In 2003-2004, Prof Bernhard Winking
Architekten added a sensitive extension
to the rear, a cubic structure (right)
that alludes to Schumacher's prewar
Hamburg — he acted as Head Construction
Director from 1909 to 1933, lending
the city its clinker-brick character. The
extension adds large windows and a top
storey, giving the policemen a better
viewpoint over their rowdy precinct.
Davidstrasse, www.davidwache-hamburg.de

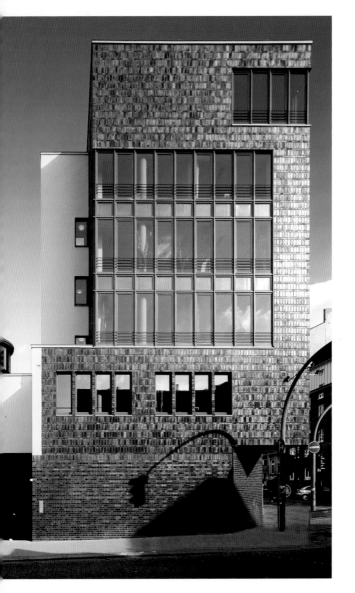

Elbberg Campus

Another work by local studio BRT, Elbberg Campus is a modular, open-plan complex of lofts and workspaces. Situated behind the Habitat store (see p066), at the base of a steep, grassy cliff, it overlooks the harbour's hotchpotch of warehouses and BRT's Dockland building (see p010). The exteriors match their surroundings: on the south side a glass façade reflects light and the water, while the land-facing north side is clad in green copper. The architects have managed to cram four storeys of floor space into a difficult, wedge-shaped site. The buildings connect further to the surrounding environment with landscaped stairs and walkways, which create a self-contained meeting point on the hillside.
Elbberg 8-10, www.elbbergcampusaltona.de

View Point

Local practice Renner Hainke Wirth was inspired by a periscope 'emerging from the depths and scanning the horizon' when conceiving this striking, 13m-high observation tower, located by the cruise liner terminal. From the top, visitors can peruse the work in progress at HafenCity; there's a particularly good panorama of Kaispeicher A, which will become Herzog & de Meuron's Elbphilharmonie (see p024)

or wave off travellers on the 60 ships that depart from here each year. View Point's 12 tonnes of steel have been clad in orange plate and cookie-cut into irregular shapes on the viewing platform. The nearby Cruise Centre is by the same studio. The main walls of this simple structure are formed from stacked ship containers, while a glass façade looks out to View Point.
Kibbelsteg, www.hafencity.com

Staatsoper

Hamburg's opera house dates back more than 300 years (its first incarnation was a shed-like affair), and over the centuries luminaries such as Richard Wagner and Gustav Mahler have graced its stage. Distel and Grubitz's art deco building, the basic structure of which you see today, was completed in 1926, but its auditorium was destroyed in WWII. The Bauhaus architect Gerhard Weber rebuilt it in 1955, and a concrete-and-glass annexe was added by Kleffel Köhnholdt and Partners in 2005. It is home to the State Opera, the Hamburg Ballet and the Hamburg Philharmonic State Orchestra – until the latter moves to its new HafenCity home in 2010.
Grosse Theaterstrasse 25, T 35 680
www.hamburgische-staatsoper.de

Habitat

BRT has no less than three major works on the small stretch of land between Van-der-Smissen-Strasse and the Altonaer Balkon. Located between Dockland (see p010) and Elbberg Campus (see p062) is the firm's design for this Habitat store. Shaped like a container ship, the building sits at the base of a landscaped park near the riverbank, and a spacious wooden terrace on the roof offers wonderful views of the harbour. More cutting-edge retail architecture can be seen further along Grosse Elbstrasse at Stilwerk (see p072), a malt factory converted into a design and lifestyle emporium.

Grosse Elbstrasse 264, T 3576 5860

Dock 47

Vivid, asymmetrical Dock 47 springs out of the flat St Pauli landscape like a flame. This dynamic office building by Spengler Wiescholek Architekten Stadtplaner stands at a busy road intersection almost directly opposite the 300-year-old Fischmarkt, and the interplay between the two is a striking metaphor for new and old Hamburg. *Pinnasberg 47, www.dock47.de*

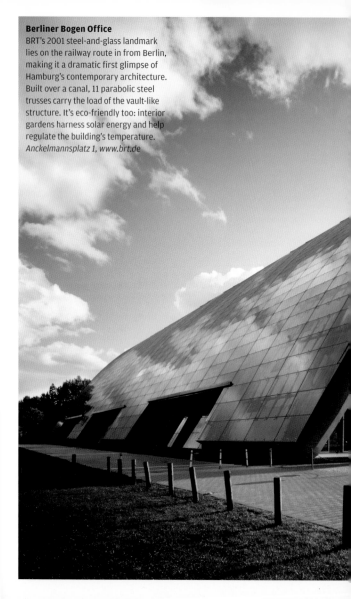

Berliner Bogen Office
BRT's 2001 steel-and-glass landmark lies on the railway route in from Berlin, making it a dramatic first glimpse of Hamburg's contemporary architecture. Built over a canal, 11 parabolic steel trusses carry the load of the vault-like structure. It's eco-friendly too: interior gardens harness solar energy and help regulate the building's temperature.
Anckelmannsplatz 1, www.brt.de

SHOPPING

THE BEST RETAIL THERAPY AND WHAT TO BUY

Almost as soon as you touch down in Hamburg, you will realise the locals are in love with shopping. There are more department stores here than in any other city in Germany, the best being Alsterhaus (Jungfernstieg 16-20, T 359 010). The city centre is the main retail hub, along pedestrianised Spitalerstrasse, upmarket Jungfernstieg, and Mönckebergstrasse, the city's 'shopping mile'. At Neuer Wall, big guns, such as local fashion maven Jil Sander (No 43, T 374 1290) and Hermès (No 40, T 351 0220), are tucked together in a pretty arcade. And at Hohe Bleichen you'll come across Petra Teufel (No 13, T 3786 1610), which stocks the likes of Paul Smith and Yohji Yamamoto. Kaufrausch (Isestrasse 74, T 480 8313) is the city's answer to Colette in Paris, and one of the many eclectic boutiques in the upscale, residential district Eppendorf.

Although a touch gritty, the Schanze area throws up some real retail gems, such as Ladenatelier (Turnerstrasse 7, T 4328 0772), which sells recycled glassware, and the fashion designer Anna Fuchs (see p086). After buying one of her fabulous frocks or coats, head down the road to It (Marktstrasse 113, T 8895 1883), where Inga Thomas will complete your outfit with the perfect pair of handmade shoes. For more fashion and interior design, head to Altona to visit Stilwerk (Grosse Elbstrasse 68, T 3062 1100), a mall of cutting-edge shops located in a converted malt factory. *For full addresses, see Resources.*

Aurim

Myths and legends are the inspiration for André Kröger's jewellery – solid, medieval-style pieces that he displays in diorama-like cabinets in his shop in the Eppendorf district. His leitmotif is the flaming heart, but he also uses crosses, playing cards, sabres and other esoterica in exquisite pendants, rings, cufflinks and earrings. Pieces are made from gold and silver, embellished with gems, crystals and pearls, and crafted in situ at his workbench in the shop. Prices are reasonable considering the quality, with a pair of silver earrings starting at £180.
Klosterallee 104, T 463 703, www.aurim.de

Koppel 66

This renovated arcade is Hamburg's hub for arts and crafts. Highlights include the playful prints of Tita do Rêgo Silva (T 2805 0599), the elegant wood-turned fountain pens of Stefan Fink (T 247 151), produced in his workshop (pictured), and handcrafted men's brogues by Annabelle Stephan (T 248 0101). Refuel at the courtyard Café Koppel (T 249 235).
Koppel 66, T 4327 0934, www.koppel66.de

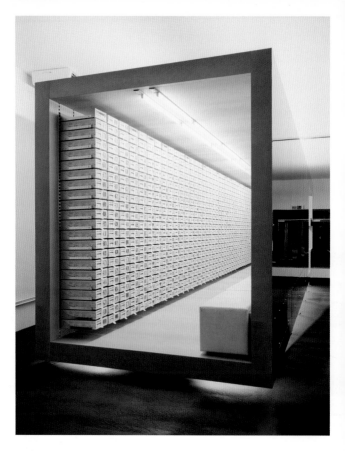

Freitag

Established in 1993, Swiss firm Freitag was the first company to recycle truck tarpaulins, turning them into stylish bags, sacks and covers for laptops and iPods. Hamburg is home to one of its three flagship stores (the others are in Zurich, the company's hometown, and Davos). Oxidised metal storage systems display smaller items, but the space is dominated by an elevated walk-in 'box', created by local firm Blauraum Architekten, containing hundreds of drawers. Each one shows an example of a different design on the front. Decide on the one you want, then start rifling through – every item is unique. Prices start at around £35 for a shopper. *Klosterwall 9, T 328 7020, www.freitag.ch*

Elternhaus

Maegde und Knechte's customised tees have a cult following in German-speaking countries. In Hamburg, their shop in the boho Marktstrasse is reminiscent of a hunting lodge, with hardwood floors and antique furniture. It contains a large range of men's and women's T-shirts (from £21), all printed with a Jenny Holzer-ish quote. Second-hand shirts and jackets – many stylishly refashioned from army surplus clothing – are similarly embellished. To complement the urban guerrilla look, there's a range of jewellery, including rings and necklaces in the shape of hand grenades, as well as chunky pendants.
Marktstrasse 29, T 430 8830,
www.elternhaus.com

Pension für Produkte

A talented group of indigenous industrial designers with a keen eye for quality, artistic vision and a sense of humour produces Pension für Produkte's range of utilitarian objects. Their showroom/warehouse near the Feldstrasse U-Bahn has a small retail section at the front. One of their best-selling products is 'Schilfstöpsel', a bath plug with a long plastic reed attached. To go with it, pick up a 'Gänsehaut' toiletry bag, £13, fashioned out of rubber bathing caps, or a 'Hans im Glück', £19, a beach towel that doubles as a stylish bag. Exclusive to the St Pauli shop is the 'Taschenlampe', £31.50, a lamp-in-a-bag, covered in a retro floral or hunting print manufactured from residues of old wallpapers.
Neuer Pferdemarkt 32, T 3803 8972, www.pensionfuerprodukte.com

Kuball & Kempe

When not acting as creative consultants for high-end manufacturers, such as Theresienthal and Deutsche Werkstätten Hellerau, style police Thomas Kuball and Peter Kempe reign over this extraordinary collection of treasures. Beautiful marble tableware from Atelier du Vieil Apt in France sits next to reissues of the famous 'Dresden Toys' by the German sculptor Richard Riemerschmid. On another shelf, covetable beauty products, such as Philip B shampoo, jostle for space with a Lalique vase, a decorative tin robot or a pair of limited-edition Adidas trainers. Tellingly, the store attracts customers from all over Europe, and many come here to pick up items from its Meissen porcelain collection: orientalist pieces exclusively reinterpreted by Kuball & Kempe.

Alter Fischmarkt 11, T 3038 2200

Sleeping Dogs

This concept store in Stilwerk (see p072) shopping mall offers carefully selected brands from Hamburg and other parts of Europe. The focus is mainly on fashion, with pieces by Maison Martin Margiela, AF Vandevorst's dangerously high 'Fetish' shoes and footwear from Zeha, a German company with a classic sports heritage. Other goodies include chocolate from In't Veld and pared-down bags, belts and bedwear by Fluo. The sexiest thing on two wheels is the 'nu Bike', the minimalist, single-speed city bicycles made in St Pauli. All these delights are displayed in a bone-white, gallery-like space, softened by tree-motif murals and cacti 'gardens'.
Stilwerk, Grosse Elbstrasse 68,
T 3861 4044, www.sleepingdogs.de

Wohnkultur 66

This furniture warehouse in the former slaughterhouse district specialises in 20th-century Scandinavian design. Its raison d'être is one man, the late Danish master craftsman Finn Juhl. Owners Martina Münch and Manfred Werner, who describe discovering Juhl's work as a life-altering experience, are the sole distributors of his furniture in Germany and one of only a handful of authorised distributors worldwide. The pieces are still made to exacting standards and production is extremely limited. Prices reflect this, though with his more iconic pieces, such as the 'Pelican' chair, reaching five figures at auction, they make a solid investment. *Sternstrasse 66, T 436 002, www.wohnkultur66.de*

Herr von Eden

Modern-day dandies will adore the sharp cuts and retro styling that mark out this German menswear label. A little bit cabaret and a little bit rock'n'roll, Herr von Eden's narrow-lapelled suits, which can be tailored to measure, come in lush velvets, fine wools and jaunty seersuckers. Shirts start at £60 and are made from fine cotton or shantung silk in a rich range of deep jewel colours.

Womenswear is limited, but if a smoking suit à la Marlene takes your fancy, this is the place to find it. The wood-lined, multi-roomed store in trendy Schanzenviertel/ Karolinenviertel (T 439 0057) evokes a Weimar gentleman's outfitters, while the new store in St Georg (above) has simple white walls and velvet-lined fixtures.
Lang Reihe 103, T 359 600 940, www.herrvoneden.com

D'Or

Along this chichi strip of Eppendorf's high street, this unusual shop has four distinct sections, each with different owners. At the front, you'll find jewellery by Warinka von Saucken (T 463 947) and an eclectic range of shoes (T 4688 1881) by designers such as Pedro García, L'Autre Chose and Sigerson Morrison. The rear is reserved for Tobias Scholl's art deco and 20th-century antiques (T 4688 1974), from Belgian ceramics and French porcelain to paste jewellery, and his own furniture line. In-between is a section dedicated to vintage designer fashion – head here for a classic Jil Sander blazer (increasingly hard to find since the label was bought out by Prada).
Eppendorfer Baum 6, T 4688 1963

Anna Fuchs

Poised on the edge of greatness, Anna Fuchs has been nominated twice for New York Fashion Week's Rising Star Award. She is big on frocks reminiscent of 1940s styles – belted, nipped and flowing creations in crêpes and silk jersey – and makes coats inspired by the golden age of Dior, and a small range of knitwear.
Karolinenstrasse 27, T 4018 5408, www.annafuchs.de

SPORTS AND SPAS

WORK OUT, CHILL OUT OR JUST WATCH

Even if you are not a member of one of the city's many exclusive sports clubs, such as Der Club An der Alster (Hallerstrasse 91, T 4142 4130), active pursuits in Hamburg are not hard to come by, thanks to the abundance of water and green space. Running is hugely popular, and early in the morning hundreds of locals don their Nikes and head to the shores of the Aussenalster to jog around the 7.5km of the Alsterrunde. If you're time-challenged, you could call TouristJogging (T 439 8780, www.touristjogging.de), which organises individual and group tours of the city's main sights on the run. And if you want a sophisticated swim, head to the landmark Alster-Schwimmhalle (Ifflandstrasse 21, T 188 890), a dramatic 1973 building designed by architect Walter Neuhäusser.

Hamburg is the home of Nivea, and Nivea Haus (Jungfernstieg 51, T 8222 4740), which opened in 2006, offers massages, facials and all kinds of well-being treatments. Other good spas include Club Olympus Spa & Fitness (opposite) and East Mandarin Body & Soul at East hotel (see p021). Calm – The Yoga Spa (Falkenried Areal, Strassenbahnring 15, T 4600 9250) was Germany's first yoga spa; you can pop in using a day pass for classes or book ahead for massages and aromatherapy in stylish surrounds. For a good old-fashioned scrub-down, try the Turkish delight that is Das Hamam in Hamburg (Feldstrasse 39, T 4135 9112).

For full addresses, see Resources.

Club Olympus Spa & Fitness

The Park Hyatt offers a limited number of memberships and day passes (£32) to its exclusive spa. Like the rest of the hotel, it stands out for its contemporary design and spaciousness. White interiors are accented with dark wood furniture, and the 20m indoor pool (above), mosaicked with lime-green and aqua tiles, should appease serious swimmers. After working out in the state-of-the-art gym, make use of the sauna, steam bath and jacuzzi, have a Swedish massage or *tuina* – a combination of acupressure and shiatsu – or book one of the beauty treatments, which use Decléor products. Packages start at £126 for a mani-pedi, there's a 90-minute treatment and lunch, and a full day's pampering is £286; a men's package is also on offer for £172.

Park Hyatt, Bugenhagenstrasse 8,
T 3332 1234, www.hamburg.park.hyatt.com

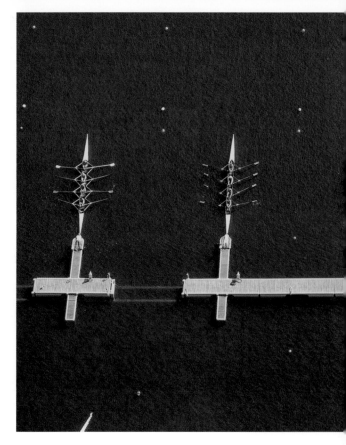

Rowing and sailing

Logically, much of Hamburg's sporting life takes place on the water. In 2004, the FISA World Masters Rowing Regatta was held on a purpose-built course on the Dove Elbe canal (pictured). The city has a proud watersports tradition and the oldest rowing club in Germany, Der Hamburger und Germania Ruder Club (T 448 794), was founded here in 1836. It's open to members only, but you can sail by its yellow boathouse, located on the Aussenalster, by hiring a boat from Bobby Reich (T 487 824). For a jaunt around the city's canals followed by lunch, pick up a canoe at the fish restaurant Goldfisch (T 5700 9690). Or in Eppendorf, Bootshaus Silwar (T 476 207) hires out boats from an estuary in the middle of a park.

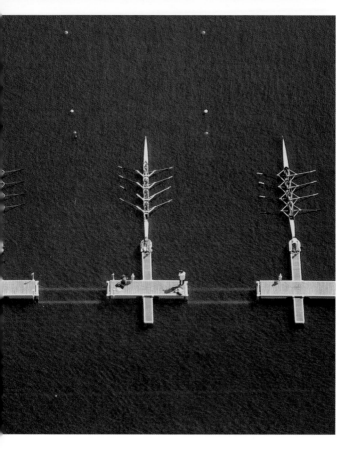

HSH Nordbank Arena
The home ground of Hamburger SV and
now also a concert venue, the Nordbank
Arena was redesigned by local firm Mos
Architekten to turn it into one of the 12
host stadiums for the 2006 World Cup.
Its capacity was boosted to 55,000 and
a state-of-the-art media centre and 50
luxurious private boxes were added.
*Sylvesterallee 7, Volkspark, T 4155 1550,
www.hsv-hshnordbank-arena.de*

Golf Lounge

Located by a canal east of HafenCity, Golf Lounge has a series of putting greens and a driving range with 30 covered practice bays, which are attractively lit up at night (above). Buy a prepaid guest card to shoot 50 balls or a rechargeable card that allows you to hit up to 1,600 balls. Lessons are also available. The stylish bar and coffee lounge does a fine line in chill-out music and cocktails, and hosts parties during events. Alternatively, visit one of the city's many golf courses, such as the pay-and-play Red Golf Hamburg-Moorfleet (T 788 7720), which has an attractive wooden clubhouse. *Billwerder Neuer Deich 40, T 8197 8790, www.golflounge.info*

ESCAPES

WHERE TO GO IF YOU WANT TO LEAVE TOWN

Autobahns with no speed limits and a very efficient train system enhance the pleasure of jaunts out of Hamburg. The high-speed ICE train (www.bahn.de) connects to Berlin in around 90 minutes, while more bucolic pursuits can be found in the outlying villages and towns. Blankenese (which can be reached on the S-Bahn local train) is the region's most picturesque village, situated on a hill overlooking the Elbe. Less than an hour by train from Hamburg, Lübeck (www.luebeck-tourismus.de) still conjures up some of the splendour it enjoyed as capital of the Hanseatic League in the 14th century, despite the rebuilding after WWII. While here, visit the museums of three heavyweights of German culture: the baroque Buddenbrookhaus (Mengstrasse 4, T 045 1122 4190) is the childhood home of Heinrich and Thomas Mann, and the Günter Grass-Haus (Glockengiesserstrasse 21, T 045 1122 4231) shows the writer's early work as a sculptor and painter. Have lunch in the medieval dining room of the Schiffergesellschaft (Breite Strasse 2, T 045 176 770), which charmingly translates as 'guild of the blue water captains'.

Sylt (www.meer-sylt.de), otherwise known as the 'Hamptons of Germany', is three hours' drive from Hamburg and the most famous of the North Sea islands. Once a refuge for poets and painters, it's now where the stylish set comes for its long, pristine (often nudist) beaches, thatched cottages and designer shops.

For full addresses, see Resources.

Kempinski Grand Hotel, Heiligendamm
Three hours by train from Hauptbahnhof Süd, *Die weisse Stadt am Meer* (or 'The White Town By The Sea') was Germany's first spa town, designed for emperors and European kingpins to take in some sea air in luxurious seclusion. Fast-forward more than 200 years and heads of state are still congregating here; Heiligendamm played host to the 2007 G8 summit. The leaders met in the six palaces that make up the Kempinski Grand Hotel, which the group opened in 2003 after years of extensive renovation work. Pictured above are three of them: the Kurhaus (left), the hub of the resort's social life with elegant restaurants overlooking the Baltic; Haus Mecklenburg (centre) and Hohenzollern Castle (right). Facilities include an in-house yoga master. *Prof-Dr-Vogel-Strasse 16-18, T 038 203 7400, www.kempinski-heiligendamm.com*

Hotel de Rome, Berlin

If you decide to stay overnight in Berlin, we suggest that you book a room in the sumptuous Hotel de Rome, located in a former bank in the Bebelplatz district. This classic Prussian building, dating from 1889, was remodelled using a palette of mushroom, coffee, black and oxblood by interior designer Tommaso Ziffer. If retail therapy is part of your plan after checking in (we recommend the first-floor mahogany-panelled suites), head to concept store Strange Fruit (overleaf; T 030 2061 4255), where cult designers such as Anne Valérie Hash and Richard Nicoll are displayed in a minimalist interpretation of a great Parisian fashion house. For lunch or dinner, the upmarket steakhouse Grill Royal (T 030 2887 9288) is a hot ticket, trawling in the beautiful people with its decadent, old Berlin vibe.
Behrenstrasse 37, T 030 460 6090, www.hotelderome.com

Strange Fruit, Berlin

Houseboats, Hvide Sande, Denmark
Denmark's proximity to north Germany makes it a popular escape, and these simple yet stylish houseboats are little more than three hours' drive away. Anchored on the Ringkøbing Fjord, a majestic wetland and bird sanctuary in the West Jutland district, the five floating homes were designed by the Århus-based firm Cubo Arkitekter. Each lower deck holds a kitchen/family room, one or two double bedrooms and two verandas. On the upper deck, the living room overlooks the fjord, and there's a veranda with space for a barbecue. Cubo have also designed nine houseboats at Bork Havn (00 45 75 280 344) further south on the same fjord. Weekly rental starts at £295 in low season for a boat with three bedrooms.
Feriepartner, Nørregade 2b, T 00 45 96 593 593, www.hvidesande-feriehuse.dk

NOTES

SKETCHES AND MEMOS

RESOURCES

CITY GUIDE DIRECTORY

HOTELS

ADDRESSES AND ROOM RATES

25hours 017
Room rates:
double, €105;
Large Standard Room, €105;
Room 500, €105-120
Paul-Dessau-Strasse 2
T 855 070
www.25hours-hotel.com

Hotel Atlantic Kempinski 018
Room rates:
double, from €295;
BMW Suite, from €4,900
An der Alster 72-79
T 28 880
www.kempinski.atlantic.de

Cap San Diego 016
Room rates:
double, €90
Überseebrücke
T 364 209
www.capsandiego.de

East 021
Room rates:
double, from €170;
Room 116, from €170;
East Apartment, from €395
Simon-von-Utrecht-Strasse 31
T 309 930
www.east-hamburg.de

Fairmont Hotel Vier Jahreszeiten 016
Room rates:
double, €300
Neuer Jungfernstieg 9-14
T 34 940
www.fairmont.com/hamburg

Gastwerk Hotel 023
Room rates:
double, from €130;
Junior Suite, from €180;
Conran Shop Suite, €270;
Penthouse Suite, €270
Beim Alten Gaswerk 3
Daimlerstrasse
T 890 620
www.gastwerk.com

Kempinski Grand Hotel 097
Room rates:
double, from €135
Prof-Dr-Vogel-Strasse 16-18
Bad Doberan
Heiligendamm
T 038 203 7400
www.kempinski-heiligendamm.com

Hotel Louis C Jacob 030
Room rates:
double, €255
Elbchaussee 401-403
T 822 550
www.hotel-jacob.de

Mövenpick Hotel 016
Room rates:
double, from €140
Sternschanze 6
T 334 4110
www.wasserturm-schanzenpark.de

Park Hyatt 016
Room rates:
double, from €255
Bugenhagenstrasse 8
T 3332 1234
hamburg.park.hyatt.com

Radisson SAS Hotel 014
Room rates:
double, from €110
Marseiller Strasse 2
T 35 020
www.hamburg.radissonsas.com

Hotel de Rome 098
Room rates:
double, from €250;
suites, from €450
Behrenstrasse 37
Berlin
T 030 460 6090
www.hotelderome.com

Side 020
Room rates:
double, from €160;
Executive Suite, from €235;
XXL Suite 1109, €610
Drehbahn 49
T 309 990
www.side-hamburg.de

Hotel Village 016
Room rates:
double, from €95
Steindamm 4
T 480 6490
www.hotel-village.de

Hotel Wedina 022
Room rates:
double, from €110;
Room 312, from €150
Gurlittstrasse 23
T 280 8900
www.wedina.de

Hotel York 016
Room rates:
double, from €98
Hofweg 19
T 227 1420
www.hotel-york.de

YoHo 016
Room rates:
double for under-26s, from €85;
double for over-26s, €115
Moorkamp 5
T 284 1910
www.yoho-hamburg.de

WALLPAPER* CITY GUIDES

Editorial Director
Richard Cook

Art Director
Loran Stosskopf
City Editor
Suzanne Wales
Editor
Rachael Moloney
Executive Managing Editor
Jessica Firmin
Travel Bookings Editor
Sara Henrichs

Chief Designer
Daniel Shrimpton
Designer
Lara Collins
Map Illustrator
Russell Bell

Photography Editor
Christopher Lands
Photography Assistant
Robin Key

Chief Sub-Editor
Jeremy Case
Sub-Editor
Vicky McGinlay
Assistant Sub-Editor
Milly Nolan
Editorial Assistant
Ella Marshall

**Wallpaper* Group
Editor-in-Chief**
Tony Chambers
Publisher
Neil Sumner

Contributors
Christopher Patterson
Meirion Pritchard
Ellie Stathaki

Wallpaper* ® is a
registered trademark
of IPC Media Limited

All prices are correct at
time of going to press,
but are subject to change.

PHAIDON

Phaidon Press Limited
Regent's Wharf
All Saints Street
London N1 9PA

Phaidon Press Inc
180 Varick Street
New York, NY 10014

Phaidon® is a registered
trademark of Phaidon
Press Limited

www.phaidon.com

First published 2008
© 2008 IPC Media Limited

ISBN 978 0 7148 4740 5

A CIP Catalogue record for
this book is available from
the British Library.

Printed in China

PHOTOGRAPHERS

Ralf Buscher
Dock 47, pp068-069

Klaus Frahm
Dat Backhus, p025

Oliver Heissner/Artur
View Point, p063
HSH Nordbank
Arena, pp092-093

**Sabine Lubeuow/
Look-foto**
Kempinski Grand Hotel,
Heiligendamm, p097

**Aufwind-Luftbilder/
VISUM**
Rowing and sailing,
pp090-091

Gulliver Theis
Club La Nuit, pp052-053

Patrick Voigt
Dockland, pp010-011
Chilehaus, p013
Congress Centrum
Hamburg, p014
Die Herren Simpel, p033
Köhlbrandbrücke, p057
Elbberg Campus, p062
Staatsoper, pp064-065
Habitat, pp066-067

Markus Wendler
Hamburg city view,
inside front cover
Flakturm IV, p012
Rathaus, p015
Hotel Wedina, p022
HafenCity, pp026-027
Lime Tree
Terrace, p030
Bistrot Vienna, p031
Café Paris, pp034-035
Tide, pp036-037
Henssler &
Henssler, p038
Cox Restaurant, p039
R&B, pp040-041
Yakshi's Bar and East
Restaurant, p042
Tarantella, p043
Tafelhaus, pp044-045
A Mora, pp046-047
Bar Rossi, pp050-051
Christopher
Patterson, p055
ADA 1, pp058-059
Berliner Bogen
Office, pp070-071
Aurim, p073
Koppel 66, pp074-075
Elternhaus, p077
Pension für Produkte,
pp078-079
Kuball & Kempe, p080
Herr von Eden, p084
D'Or, p085
Anna Fuchs, pp086-087

HAMBURG
A COLOUR-CODED GUIDE TO THE HOT 'HOODS

EIMSBÜTTEL
This pretty, tree-lined residential district is becoming increasingly hip as creatives move in

ST GEORG
The gay village is alive with clubs, cinemas, boutiques, and boating on the Aussenalster

MITTE WEST
This classy central district is home to shops, cafés and the Planten un Blomen gardens

EPPENDORF AND HARVESTEHUDE
A bourgeois haven of upmarket retailers and refined classical and neo-baroque mansions

HAFENCITY
Massive docklands redevelopment and investment here is invigorating the entire city

SCHANZE
Find funky delis and fashion start-ups in this alternative district centred on Marktstrasse

MITTE EAST
The central retail hub is also home to swathes of vernacular clinker-brick office buildings

ALTONA AND ST PAULI
This multifaceted zone boasts cutting-edge architecture, strip clubs and gourmet shops

For a full description of each neighbourhood, see the Introduction.
Featured venues are colour-coded, according to the district in which they are located.